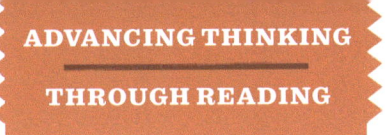

I0555438

Bananas

First, Second, Third...

Lauren Johnson
Illustrated by Mek Frinchaboy

ISBN: 979-8-218-29404-5

Printed in USA
Published by Jackrabbit Books

Today, I went to the market and got a perfect yellow banana. I wonder how this banana got here? Let's find out!

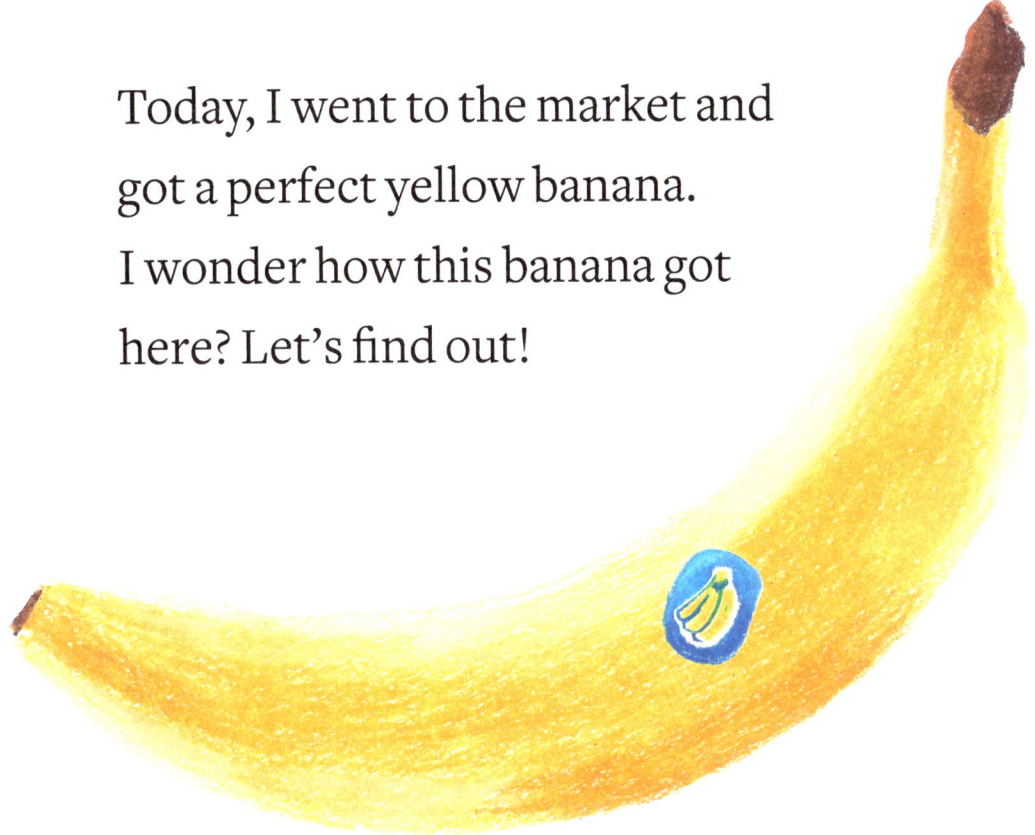

First, the banana farmer digs a deep hole in the dirt. There are two ways to plant a banana tree. One way is to plant a seed. Banana seeds look like little stones.

This is its real size.

Another way is to cut a small branch—called a sucker—from a banana tree and plant *that* in the ground.

3

Then, the sun shines down and warms the seed. The sunlight and the rain give the seed energy to grow. They provide the seed with the water and nutrients it needs to grow.

Second, the tree trunk starts to grow. Over time, it gets bigger and taller, and bunches of bananas start to sprout from the trunk. One tree can produce over 200 bananas.

Most trees take
ten years to grow,
but a banana tree
can grow in only
nine months!

7

Third, when the bananas are dark green, the farmer picks them. They are not ready to be eaten yet, though. Then the bananas are washed, checked, and packed.

Did you know a bunch of bananas is called a hand, and one banana is called a finger? Isn't that funny?

Fourth, the banana farmers put the newly-picked green bananas in big boxes. The boxes are loaded onto a refrigerated truck which drives along the road until it reaches a ship docked in the water.

Fifth, the boxes are moved from the truck to the ship. The ship transports the bananas across the ocean. The bananas are stored in large, refrigerated containers on the ship. Bananas must stay cool, about the temperature of a chilly fall day.

Sixth, the ship moves across the water and docks in a new town. The dockworkers unload the boxes of bananas on the dock.

The biggest container ship can hold up to 745 million bananas. That is more than one banana for every person in America!

15

Seventh, the bananas are moved from the dock to another truck, or to a refrigerated train. This trip ends with the bananas being brought to a special place called a "cooling building," where they can ripen and turn from dark green to light yellow.

Did you know that bananas are ranked on a scale of 1–7 for ripeness? 7 = dark green and 1 = bright yellow with little brown spots.

Eighth, when the bananas have ripened from the cooling building, the workers move the banana bunches to a truck again. Sometimes, they send green bananas to the store, but usually they give them time to ripen to yellow.

Now they
are yellow!

Ninth, the bananas arrive at the market. The truck is unloaded, and workers place the bananas on the shelves to be bought. This is the end of their journey.

Tenth, my bright yellow, perfect banana is bought and brought home. Hooray!

More than 96% of American households buy bananas at least once a month.

Finally, snack time is here!

I choose my perfect banana and eat it up!

Bananas have many
vitamins and minerals,
like potassium, that build
a healthy body and a
healthy mind!

Your Turn #1

Here are the transitional time and sequence terms in the book. How many of these words can you use in a sentence?

- First
- Second
- Third
- Fourth
- Fifth
- Sixth
- Seventh
- Eighth
- Ninth
- Tenth
- Then
- Finally

Your Turn #2

Fill in the blanks below.

1. When I wake up in the morning, the first thing I do is

   _____

2. When I wake up in the morning, the second thing I do is

   _____

3. When I wake up in the morning, the third thing I do is

   _____

4. After lunch, I like to

   _____

5. Finally, before I go to bed, I like to

   _____

NOTE TO PARENTS & TEACHERS

When early learners hear and see transitional words and phrases in context, they will use them in their writing and vocabulary. This book gives young scholars a jump-start on language acquisition and non-fiction content knowledge to support comprehension, speaking, listening, and writing skills.

www.ingramcontent.com/pod-product-compliance
Lightning Source LLC
Chambersburg PA
CBHW041440120626
46547CB00002B/288